SAVING THE QUEEN

Borgo Press Books by THÉOPHILE GAUTIER

Saving the Queen (with Bernard Lopez)

SAVING THE QUEEN

A COMEDY OF
CAPE AND SWORD

THÉOPHILE GAUTIER

& BERNARD LOPEZ

Adapted and Translated by Frank J. Morlock

THE BORGO PRESS
MMXIII

SAVING THE QUEEN

Copyright © 2006, 2013 by Frank J. Morlock

FIRST BORGO PRESS EDITION

Published by Wildside Press LLC

www.wildsidebooks.com

DEDICATION

To My Dear Friend, Tony Smith

CONTENTS

CAST OF CHARACTERS 9
ACT I: The First Day 11
ACT II: The Second Day 49
ACT III: The Third Day 117
ALTERNATIVE ENDING 151
ABOUT THE TRANSLATOR 155

CAST OF CHARACTERS

Don Melchior de Bovadilla, a ruined young gentleman

Don Gaspar, soldier of fortune

Count de San Lucas, Grand Master of Ceremony and uncle of Don Melchior and Doña Beatrix

Hilario, page

Rafael, page

A Head of the Alguazils (the Bailiffs)

Elizabeth Farnese, Queen of Spain

Doña Beatrix d'Astorga, Lady of Honor

Griselda, The Queen's Lady of Chamber

ACT I
THE FIRST DAY

A place in the park of Aranjuez; a pavilion on each side.

At the back a raised terrain that is usable.

Count de San Lucas

What's that uproar, what's going on—is that my niece's voice?

Doña Beatrix (running)

Help! Help!

Count de San Lucas

What is it?

Doña Beatrix

The Queen—

Count de San Lucas

Well—?

Doña Beatrix

Her horse is running away.

Count de San Lucas

Great God!

Doña Beatrix

It's dragging her through the fields in the direction of the Tagus River.

Count de San Lucas

May our Lady be in aid of Her Gracious Majesty; I make verses for her salvation as is the duty of all faithful subjects.

Doña Beatrix

It's not a question of that! Run! Fly! Perhaps there's no more time. Each second that is wasted shortens the life of Her Majesty by a year!

Count de San Lucas

I actually told our charming sovereign to beware of

this black horse that she always insists on mounting—instead of the traditional hackney—but now they treat me as an old fool, as a gothic dotard.

Doña Beatrix

You are making me die with impatience, with your measured phrases! What, gentlemen, and you are a bunch of gentlemen, young, strong, and bold—your Queen, a woman—is in peril and you don't budge.

Count de San Lucas

If she was only a woman, ten of us would already have rushed—but the Queen, that's altogether different.

Doña Beatrix

What do you mean?

Count de San Lucas

All men who touch the Queen, even to save her—are punished by death. That's a well-known law of Spain.

Doña Beatrix

Save the Queen and die!

Count de San Lucas

I have too great a respect for etiquette, and too much

love for life! Besides, as grand-master of ceremonies I must avoid doing anything against the rules. That would be an irritating precedent—a veritable scandal!

Doña Beatrix

My God! My God!— What to do? Eh, what—no one can decide? O chevaliers of Spain, land of courage and gallantry—so this is what you've come to: there's not one heart under these doublets? What must I say to persuade you?— My voice is breaking, my mind is wandering—ah, the one who will save my mistress—I shall love him like a brother, like a spouse.

Count de San Lucas

My niece—calm this irregular...exaltation.

Doña Beatrix

I will give him my heart.

Count de San Lucas

Niece!

Doña Beatrix

My hand!

Count de San Lucas

Niece! Recollect that you are my ward, and that I have kept your hand—for my nephew Don Melchior, that I am bringing expressly from Granada to marry you off, and he ought to arrive today— Gentlemen, don't listen to her.

Doña Beatrix

Hear me, mercy—if you are Spaniards—if you are gentlemen—at this moment perhaps your Queen is dying.

Count de San Lucas

Ah, here's Griselda, the chamber maid—perhaps we shall learn—

(Griselda enters.)

Griselda

Good news, gentlemen— The Queen isn't dead!

Count de San Lucas

Long live the Queen!

Griselda

It's a miracle—she doesn't even have a scratch.

Doña Beatrix

Unhoped-for blessing!—I thank heaven for it!

Count de San Lucas

An explosion of joy would not be out of place at this moment, I laugh I jump—I toss my hat in the air!

(He remains motionless)

Doña Beatrix

O my dear Mistress— Speak, Griselda—how was she able to escape this danger?

Count de San Lucas

Despite the distance that separates us, I am myself interrogating a simple serving girl—Griselda— Tell us—

Griselda

Gladly—I begin—It's a question of a young man—

Doña Beatrix

Ah!

Griselda

What am I saying?—better than that—

Count de San Lucas

Of a man of ripe age?

Griselda

No—of two young men—two valiants, two heroes who did not fear to expose their lives to save their Queen.

Doña Beatrix

Two?

Count de San Lucas

There you are, niece, in a fine fix—your imprudent promise forces you to be a perjurer or a bigamist.

Doña Beatrix

Eh! What?— Wasn't one able to know which?

Griselda

You get lost in conjecture They were seen running, one after the other in the same direction and then the thickness of the woods concealed them from our view; shouts could be heard.

Don Diego de Escalona, the squire who was advanced further than the rest of the suite, stopped suddenly as if struck into a stupor.

Count de San Lucas

I hope that nothing contrary to etiquette took place in this terrible moment—for a queen, it's better to die than to be drawn from peril in an inconvenient way—what happened?

Griselda

Don Diego d'Escalona just saw a young man stopping the horse of Her Majesty.

Count de San Lucas

Shocking situation and outside all established rules.

Doña Beatrix

Noble heart.

Griselda

Alas, that's not all—Don Diego also saw the Queen slip from her saddle, her foot caught in the stirrup.

Doña Beatrix

Great God!

Griselda

And the wretched young man seized her in his arms.

Count de San Lucas

I grow pale and blush alternatively— to take the Queen in his arms.

Only the King of Spain can do things like that unpunished—it's an atrocious crime—a failure to know how to live that's worthy of death.

Griselda

It was two steps from a quagmire—

Doña Beatrix

The Queen had to be saved.

Count de San Lucas

Saved yes—but touched, no.

Griselda

Luckily, Milord Count, everyone is not as ceremonious as you. But for this generous inconvenience, what would have become of the Queen?

When we reached the scene of the accident, we found

her fainted at the foot of a tree!

Count de San Lucas

My sovereign at the foot of a tree—without velour cushions, without a canopy with a coat of arms? Sun—you didn't veil yourself from such a sight? And how did Her Majesty endure this unexampled calamity?

Griselda

We got her to come to with water of the Queen of Hungary—Her Majesty told us then she had seen only one man—and that in the trouble, the weakness in which she found herself—she was unable to distinguish his appearance—terror causing a syncope—he resembled vaguely some unknown who had carried her from her saddle—and bore her to a mound of lawn—after that she didn't remember a thing. I was one who informed her of the two young cavaliers who had been carried away by heroism and speed.

Doña Beatrix

What a mystery!—is one unaware what's become of them?

Count de San Lucas

Did they succeed in arresting them?

Griselda

I opine, indeed, no, Lord Count. It was the head of the Alguazils, Martínez, who is in charge of pursuing them—and everyone knows his clumsiness that is equaled only by boorishness. Still—alas— They say—

Doña Beatrix

What?

Griselda

That one of them, trying to flee, drowned in The Tagus.

Count de San Lucas

Drowned.

Doña Beatrix

May God will that not to be!

But I'm delaying to see Her Majesty—you who know where she is, Griselda—lead us!

Count de San Lucas

Yes, etiquette does not forbid us from manifesting a respectful emotion—and I follow you.

(The others leave. The Count starts to follow them but

Don Melchior enters and holds him back)

Don Melchior

One moment! Allow the worst of nephews to give an embrace to the best of uncles.

Count de San Lucas

Easy! Don Melchior de Bovadilla!—you are going to rumple my ruff—

Don Melchior

Allow me, quite unworthy though I be, to rush into your arms! It's the voice of blood that speaks—listen to it!

Count de San Lucas

That's fine! That's fine!

Don Melchior

It tells one to embrace you yet once more.

Count de San Lucas

Don Melchior, you love me too much!

Don Melchior

Oh! I feel it! I was born for the joys of the family. For the peaceable happiness of the hearth.

Count de San Lucas

So it's for that you have filled Granada with scandals—that there are rumors of your misconduct with the gypsies of Albayasin, and of your braves with Toreros in the cabarets—a singular manner of proving your taste for tranquil pleasures.

Don Melchior

Alas!—men are so nasty that they find ways of slandering even the devil! There must be a great deal of invention in the legends they've rehearsed to you of my adolescence.

Count de San Lucas

And these memorials of tradesmen, as long as you sword that and paid with my poor money—were they also inventions?

Don Melchior

Would I have paid my uncle the insult of addressing myself to others for these bagatelles? Besides, if I have debts, they were to sustain the honor of our name.

Count de San Lucas

You sustain it too well. I have settled your accounts three times.

Don Melchior

Sublime uncle!

Count de San Lucas

I am not in funds—I warn you of that—are you going to ask money of me again?

Don Melchior

Despite my youth, I no longer have illusions in that regard—the uncles of these days are such rascals they deserve to be their own nephews! Reassure yourself—I will abuse my nepotism only to request a Homeric feast.

Count de San Lucas

You are then still hungry—?

Don Melchior

I'm starving! Since leaving Granada I've only eaten in inns—and just now, I ran so hard.

Count de San Lucas

What are you saying? What suspicion? Is it you, by chance—could you have compromised yourself in this fatal adventure—?

Don Melchior

What do you mean? I would really like to be dining.

Count de San Lucas

Are you unaware that an audacious person, under the pretext of saving her, has just touched the Queen—and that's a crime punishable by death.

Don Melchior (aside)

Ah! The devil!

Count de San Lucas

Answer! Would you by chance be one of those bold cavaliers that are being accused of this sacrilegious devotion?

Don Melchior

Do you take me for the opening chapter in a novel?

A horse that bolts, a furious bull, a fainting heroine—and the inevitable young man who comes to the point of aiding her—that's the bridge of donkeys—I don't pass over that bridge. A self-respecting man leaves such exploits to students of theology—

Anyway, I don't save women—on the contrary—

Count de San Lucas

Then it wasn't you? I ought to inquire into it, my position obliges me to— And yet I also have some reasons to be afflicted by—in your interests, actually.

Don Melchior

What do you mean?

Count de San Lucas

You know how I made you come from Granada?

Don Melchior

On several very rough Mules in the midst of a cacophony of bells—but I would like to be dining—

Count de San Lucas

The question is not that—answer—

Don Melchior

Ah! Yes—you have sinister plans against me—you

were pondering marrying me.

Count de San Lucas

And you are not thanking me for it?

Don Melchior

My word, no.

Count de San Lucas

You are a simple monster of ingratitude—I destine you for your cousin—Doña Beatrix d'Astorga.

Don Melchior

On the subject—is she pretty?

Count de San Lucas

She has charming escutcheons.

Don Melchior

Is she rich—?

Count de San Lucas

Enough to make you wait patiently for my inheritance.

Don Melchior

How much?

Count de San Lucas

Two million reals.

Don Melchior

Let the priest and the notaries be called.

Count de San Lucas

Don't be in such a hurry—Doña Beatrix is lost for you.

Don Melchior

Ah! Heaven—and as for me, I have no more credit!

Count de San Lucas

That little idiot—didn't she take it into her head to promise her hand to the one who would save the queen.

Don Melchior

What are you telling me?

Count de San Lucas

If you had been this savior—I would be able to forget that I am the representative of etiquette. Even though my duty as Grand Master of Ceremonies is opposed to it, I would have solicited, begged, used my credit to obtain your pardon— One can sometimes waive from strict principals in favor of a relative.

Don Melchior

Ruined.

Count de San Lucas

And ruinous! This marriage would have fulfilled my wishes—but it must no longer be thought of—you are no longer in the situation exacted by Doña Beatrix.

Don Melchior (aside)

Ah! The devil!

(aloud)

Is it known who is the one who has rights to my beautiful cousin?

Count de San Lucas

Speculation is born on two young men—both unknown.

Don Melchior (aside)

Unknown? Very fine!

(aloud)

I am one of them.

Count de San Lucas

And we were assured that one of these eternal heroes drowned in the Tagus.

Don Melchior (aside)

Drowned! Wonderful! Uncle?

Count de San Lucas

Nephew?

Don Melchior

Perhaps you don't know to what degree I am modest?

Count de San Lucas

I hadn't noticed it.

Don Melchior

Modesty is humble quality that one glories in having—

There are others that one prides oneself on; as for me, I hide 'em—I have whole warehouses of clandestine good deeds—I have monopolies of unpublished heroics—provisions for sacrifices that have never seen the light of day—I've acted in this way so as not to humiliate my contemporaries—

Count de San Lucas

In truth?

Don Melchior

Nothing is more unbearable to me than these boasters who only know how to speak of their exploits—like these swaggerers breaking into heaven by the hook of their mustaches and that faint with fear at a bird leaping from the hay— As for me, I let my actions be my panegyric—and I'm so afraid of passing for a braggart that I might be taken for a coward.

Count de San Lucas

I admire you!

Don Melchior

Just now, when you asked me if I was the savior of the Queen, I answered no— As a consequence of this system that urges me to deprecate myself. So as not to take up the bad habits of folks who boast about everything.

Count de San Lucas

Well.

Don Melchior

I was deceiving you— The savior of the Queen—

Count de San Lucas

What?— It was you?

Don Melchior

Myself!

Count de San Lucas

And you said nothing about it?

Don Melchior

It's repugnant to proclaim myself a hero. I would leave this case to trumpets of renown.

Count de San Lucas

Simple and grand!

Don Melchior

But since you say that this act of courage puts its author in peril of death—I must name myself—my bravery exacts it—you are quite sure of getting me married, huh? Send me a verbal guarantee.

Count de San Lucas

Nephew, count on me—I will neglect nothing—I shall run to speak instantly to some influential members of the Council of Castile. While waiting, go into this pavilion.

(He opens the pavilion to the audience's left)

No one will expect to find you there.

Don Melchior (in the doorway)

That's all the same. I'd really like to dine—but to obey you—

(turning back)

One more word, uncle—is the King jealous?— Has he that inconvenient conjugal trait?

Count de San Lucas

Singular question! He's jealous like a simple lover.

Don Melchior

Then I am lost!— He will never forgive me for having known a joy whose monopoly belongs to him.

Count de San Lucas

What do you mean?

Don Melchior

This yellow dress—has it not grazed the august corsage of the Queen? May Saint Iago, the patron of valorous men, be of help to me.

(He goes inside the pavilion)

Count de San Lucas

Perhaps I'd do better to abandon him to his fate, but if he marries Beatrix, I am rid of him all the same, and that's better.

It is always deplorable for a well-situated uncle to see his nephew appear in a public place.

(He leaves—a moment later Don Gaspar, wrapped in a cloak, appears)

Don Gaspar (alone)

They've lost my track. I can breathe easy for a moment. What matter, anyway if these Alguazils succeed in arresting me. The sacrifice of my life has occurred—I cannot be happy—what's the good of dragging out a miserable existence for a long time?

I am not unaware of the approaching marriage of Doña Beatrix! If I die before it, I will have no more to endure except the cruel thought that she will belong to another. Ah! Why did I meet her on my way? Why did I notice the first time her divine features through the grilled gate of the choir—in that Convent of Burgos?— I too much forgot I am a soldier of fortune. What madness in me with only a cape and sword—to love a rich and noble heiress.

(At this moment Alguazils pass over a hill at the back. Don Gaspar hides behind a tree.)

Again those Alguazils. Oh why dispute my life with them? Is it worth the bother? I wanted to suffocate this love—I felt that reason was powerless. Doña Beatrix came to court—I followed her there, giving myself the pretext that I had to solicit a reward long since promised for my services. Rather, it was because I could not live far from her! And today again, if I got into the Park of Aranjuez, if I mixed with the royal hunt, I was still urged on by the ardent desire of seeing her— if only it were for an instant. It's my only happiness. I've never dared to accost her—to say to her: I love you! No, never!— My pride is revolted at the idea of being greeted with disdain! And what hope remains to me? Now that Doña Beatrix is the fiancée of this Don Melchior? Now especially that there's a price on my head, like that of a felon and a traitor. I touched the Queen of Spain. It's a crime of lèse-majesty! Of high treason. The Prosecutor will employ the old statutes of Don Enrique the mournful and Don Pedro the lawgiver.— And I will die!

My fate will be inevitable. How will I succeed in getting out of The Park of Aranjuez? The Alguazils have spread out on all sides— Ah—night is falling—I could, perhaps, profit from this darkness to reach some postern or to climb the walls of this enclosure. Let's attempt a last effort—and may all the Saints of Castile be my help.

(He leaves at the left. At the same moment Griselda arrives from the rear.)

Griselda (looking around her)

Over here—did the queen tell me? She saw him flee this way. Nobody.

(The Queen enters on Beatrix' arm)

Queen

Well, Griselda?

Griselda

I've searched vainly, Señora, I didn't see him.

Doña Beatrix

Allow me to mention to Your Majesty that night is

falling, that we are alone.

Queen

Who cares?— If I am distracted it's by design—I admit it to you, Beatrix—I had a plan in separating myself from the body of the hunt. A vague hope of meeting the generous stranger who was not afraid to risk his life for me.— Oh! I would so like to see him again, to thank him—

Griselda

And it's toward this part of the woods that Your Majesty saw him flee—this young hero?

Queen

That's the way it seemed to me through my faint. He didn't go, at the risk of being hanged, until my people arrived. I already feel myself an ingrate for not having expressed my gratitude to him already.

He might think that I am abandoning him to his peril— That thought is troublesome to me— On behalf of my Queen's crown, I will save him, I will reward him—I will know how to shield him from this cruel and stupid law— What will we do to those who hate us if this is the way we treat those who are devoted to us?

Doña Beatrix

Thanks, Madame, thanks for these kind and generous words—I was expecting no less from Your Majesty. You know the promise that I made. I will keep it with joy. What do I care about the name of this young man? For Beatrix d'Astorga he's called—the Savior of the Queen. There's no more beautiful title in the world.

Griselda

I would marry him eyes closed—He must be an accomplished and brave cavalier like the motto on a garter. I would bet on it! To brave death thus with gaiety of heart, that's not the work of an old man or one ill-built. Assuredly, he deserves interest for his action and his physique.

Doña Beatrix

Your Majesty will intercede for him with King Don Philippe, and your prayer will be granted, no question; the King has such affection for you—

Queen

Yes, Don Philippe cannot remain deaf to the voice of humanity. In any other country, instead of mercy I would ask for a reward. I will no doubt succeed—for I have some power over him—I will succeed if my influence doesn't break against that of Alberoni.

Doña Beatrix

Alberoni! Isn't he devoted to Your Majesty? Wasn't it he who placed you on the throne of Spain, and that we must thank for the kindness on behalf of your subjects?

Queen

If he placed me on the throne, he would already make me descend from it. Do you imagine that it was a good memory of his country that made him find me in Parma to make me the wife of Philippe the Fifth, after having driven The Princess des Ursins from Madrid? No— The lofty favorite exerted on the mind of the King an influence which made him grasp the truly prime, incontestable fact—the unarguable need that Spain experienced to have an alliance with an Italian principality.

Griselda

Oh! The old Satan! I sniff his malice. He thought the King would listen less to his wife than his mistress.

Queen

He took me for a young girl lacking will, a frivolous Italian—occupied with flowers devotions, adornments—a wife for the King and not a Queen— That's what he wanted to make of Elizabeth Farnese, Grand Duchess of Parma— He's already able to see he was deceived. Soon he tried to ruin me in the mind of the master. I met him in the way of all my plans; I found him at end of all my requests, like a locked door—and if I implore mercy, he demands punishment.

Doña Beatrix

Cussed Italian! Yet he cannot push the spirit of contradiction to the point of wanting to ruin this young man! I tremble. It must have been impossible for him to leave The Park of Aranjuez. They've placed Walloon guards and Alguazils at all the exits.

Griselda

We are playing with misfortune—here it is night already, and we are going to go back into the castle without having news of him.

(The noise of a musket shot is heard.)

Doña Beatrix

Great God!

Queen

What's happening?

(Don Gaspar enters as if pursued)

Don Gaspar

Two inches lower and I was delivered of all my worries—the bullet cut the feather off my hat.

Griselda

May my patron saint protect us! I spy a dark cloak in the black night.

Don Gaspar (aside)

I hear whispering—in feminine voices—it's not Saint Hermandad—

Griselda

Who goes there?

Don Gaspar

A distracted man.

Griselda

That's not a profession—How is it you find yourself in the park of Aranjuez after the Angelus strikes? Might you be a thief?

Don Gaspar

Ah, Señora.

Doña Beatrix

Are you a poacher?

Don Gaspar

No more.

Griselda

Then, I see no other social position for you—than lover—it's a position—nocturnal and ambulatory—

Don Gaspar

That's a less outraging hypothesis and one I can admit.

Yes, I agree, love is no stranger to my presence in this park. But now, I am running the greatest perils if I stay here— Miss, your voice is sweet, I divine you are pretty, you must be kind—indicate to me—from mercy—the path that leads to the small postern gate on the road to Bearn, I don't have a minute to lose. The Alguazils are on my track.

Queen

If it was him!

Don Gaspar

I must tell you—I committed an imprudence—fatal—

which places my life in danger.

Queen (low)

No doubt about it.

(aloud)

Explain yourself, cavalier—are you the Queen's savior?

Griselda (to Beatrix)

Now this interests you. What a shame you can't see him clearly.

Don Gaspar (aside)

Who are these women? Can I give my name?

Queen

You don't reply?

Don Gaspar

Madame—

Queen

This embarrassment makes me believe more—

Doña Beatrix

Speak—mercy—

Griselda

Count on our discretion—

Don Gaspar (aside)

These women— That's lucky.

Queen

You interest us more than you can think.

Doña Beatrix

Have no fear. We aren't the ones who will denounce you.

Griselda

We don't have lovers in the police.

Don Gaspar (aside)

Indeed, my situation cannot be worse.

Queen

Your confidence can be useful to you.

Don Gaspar

Well, yes—I admit— It was I who had the perilous honor of bringing help to Her Majesty.

Doña Beatrix

Noble young man!

Queen

Devoted heart!

Griselda

Worthy offshoot of the Cid!

Queen (going to him)

It's you—you who have no fear, to save the Queen, to expose yourself to a terrible punishment. Ah—be sure, Sir, that the Queen understands all your devotion—if she were here, she would be happy to thank you.

Don Gaspar

Who are you to know thus the feelings of the Queen?

Queen

A woman from whom Elizabeth Farnese has no secrets—one of her friends—for the Queen can have them.

(She takes Beatrix's hand)

Griselda

Be careful—I see the torches of the escort shining through the trees.

Don Gaspar

I am lost.

Queen

Not at all!— We will hide you tonight in this very palace.

Doña Beatrix

But in the meantime, my God! What to do?

Griselda

Ah! That pavilion!— Go in there!

Queen

A page will come seek you there.

(He goes into the pavilion. A moment later the Count enters with the Queen's entourage and lackeys bearing torches.)

Count de San Lucas

Over here, gentlemen. I perceive the Queen. Your carriage awaits you, Madame—with eight indispensable mules.

Queen (to a page)

Take these doubloons, Hilario!

Count de San Lucas (to another page)

Take this purse, Rafael—

Queen (pointing to the pavilion at the right)

(to Hilario)

My savior is here!

Count de San Lucas (to Rafael—pointing to the pavilion at the left)

The Queen's savior is there.

Queen (to Hilario)

You will introduce him tonight to the palace—to Griselda's apartment.

Count de San Lucas (to Rafael)

You will lead him tonight to the palace to my quarters.

Queen

To the castle, gentlemen.

Count de San Lucas

Make way for the Queen. In my capacity as general Master of Ceremonies and as gallant hidalgo, I dare throw my cloak by the path of our beautiful sovereign.

(They light the Queen's way with torches, she gives her hand to the Count, and the curtain falls)

CURTAIN

ACT II
THE SECOND DAY

Griselda's room in the castle of Aranjuez. Door at the back and left. Window to the spectator's right.

At Rise, The Queen and Doña Beatrix are seated near a table on which there are candles. Griselda looks through the door.

Queen

Well, Griselda?

Griselda

Our knight, our Amadis, hasn't arrived yet.

Doña Beatrix

I am so impatient.

Queen

Get hold of yourself, dear Beatrix, it's a good Spanish league from the rest pavilions of the hunt to the castle of Aranjuez.

Griselda (coming to the front of the stage.)

And God knows that a Spanish league is capable of wearying the patience and the legs of a saint.

Queen

Don't be afraid—I have confided this delicate mission to my faithful page, Hilario.

Griselda

I know it—he's sharp like a needle. And what reassures me further is the stupidity of the Alguazil Martínez. When he pursues others, he's the one that gets caught. And he won't have a sufficiently unlucky hand to arrest our hero.

Doña Beatrix

How hurried I am to see him! Our meeting in the woods was so absurdly interrupted by Your Majesty's escort—we don't even know his name.

Griselda

Don't worry—I bet he's at least a Medina-Coeli or a Sotomayor. You are really lucky, Doña Beatrix! As for me, I'm dying of envy to marry a noble! I'm vain enough not to think myself a morsel for a commoner.

Doña Beatrix

Madwoman! I begin to glimpse many obstacles to our union. First of all, this young cavalier already seems to be gripped by a profound and mysterious passion. And then, it's in vain that Her Majesty has already solicited mercy for him.

Queen

Yes, what I foresaw has happened—suddenly Alberoni has arrived to oppose his influence to mine.

Griselda

Cussed Italian! Ah—if instead of a servant's cap I wore the crown of a Queen—I know what I would do—

Queen

What would you do?

Griselda

I would undertake to smash Alberoni and I'd display all the shards to Europe.

Doña Beatrix

Griselda's right—why does Your Majesty allow yourself to be dominated by an adventurer, a parvenu?

Griselda

A man from nothing— At first a bell ringer at Parma then a chef for the Duke de Vendome—and who today pretends to crush through his influence a Grand Duchess of Parma.

Doña Beatrix

A queen of Spain.

Queen (rising)

We will see—the future will decide— Meanwhile, we are here obliged to watch over this poor young man!

Doña Beatrix (rising)

What are we going to do? How to get him away from his pursuers?

Griselda

That duty is my concern—it is proper that each of us do something for him. Her Majesty promises to protect him. Doña Beatrix promises to marry him—and as for me—I promise to hide him.

Doña Beatrix

Where?

Griselda

Right here.

Queen

In your chamber!

Griselda

I will answer to you for his safety as for my virtue.

Queen (smiling)

Griselda.

Doña Beatrix

The Count.

(The Count enters.)

Count de San Lucas (after bowing ceremoniously.)

Majesty—I am coming on behalf of the King! The court ball has begun. The Ambassadors of France and England will soon arrive. Etiquette demands your presence.

Queen

I am going to follow you, Señor Count—but first, tell

me—

What do you know about those two young men so gravely compromised?

Count de San Lucas

Most strict orders have been given. They will succeed, without doubt, to be recognized—and the truly guilty will be arrested.

Queen

What! You wish it?— What do you actually think of all this?

Count de San Lucas (aside)

What to say to her?

(aloud)

I will reply with frankness to Your Majesty— In the circumstance—sometimes folks to try to elude—but I who have sometimes been brutally suave—who, by profession profess the deepest respect for etiquette.

Doña Beatrix (to the Count)

Take care, uncle—the Queen in her turn wants to save her savior.

Count de San Lucas

Majesty—I see in this audacious act, a sublime exploit—

Queen

Right on, Count.

Count de San Lucas (proudly)

I've always had the courage of my opinions.

Queen

I'm deeply interested in my liberator—

Count de San Lucas

Ah, what happiness for me—I can inform you of his name.

Doña Beatrix

You know it?

Griselda

Tell us quickly.

Count de San Lucas

It's Don Melchior—my nephew.

Doña Beatrix

My cousin.

Queen

Are you sure of it?

Count de San Lucas

Oh—persuaded.

Queen

He told you?

Count de San Lucas

Swore it—and I thank heaven over it—I no longer have to fear for Beatrix a misalliance with a mysterious adventurer.

Griselda

The other hero, what became of him?

Count de San Lucas

No one knows. As for Don Melchior, thanks to the countless tact which characterizes me—I've guessed the generous intentions of Your Majesty.

Queen

What have you done?

Count de San Lucas

I charged my page Rafael to bring him to the palace tonight.

Griselda

Ah! That's like us—

Queen

This is a bizarre coincidence. Where did you actually leave him?

Count de San Lucas

In one of the rest pavilions for the hunt.

Griselda

Still like us.

Doña Beatrix

In that case, one of the two messengers cannot fail to bring him to safe port—here.

Count de San Lucas

He'll be at my place—ah, yet—

Queen

What's wrong with you?

Count de San Lucas

Despite my intense desire to please Your Majesty, I'm afraid of compromising myself by hiding him in my apartments.

Queen

I understand—and I pardon your delicacy, Señor Count! Well—you have only to give orders for Don Melchior to be immediately led here—the susceptibility of Griselda is not alarmed.

Griselda

Let him come—and by the word of a Spanish girl, I am ready to grant him an Arabian hospitality.

Queen

Then remain here, Beatrix. No question you won't be kept waiting long to see your chivalrous fiancée appear—myself, I will leave the ball for a moment to give thanks to him—come, Count. Trust me, Beatrix—I am going to put immense pressure on the King—I will have mercy for Don Melchior this evening, or I shall tomorrow solicit the ruin of Alberoni.

(She leaves with the Count.)

Griselda

Still, it's quite singular to be the fiancée of someone one doesn't know.

Doña Beatrix

Oh! I know him. My heart has foreseen him—I've already seen him my dreams—noble young man.

Griselda

But if he were ugly?

Doña Beatrix

I am sure on the contrary—beautiful souls make beautiful faces—bold with men, timid with women, sparkling eye, and sweet smile. That's the way I picture him to myself.

Griselda

As for me, what worries me is to know if he's blond or brunet.

Doña Beatrix

What's it matter?

Griselda

Brunets are passionate.

Doña Beatrix

How do you know that?

Griselda

I've noticed it—in my travels.

Doña Beatrix

Be quiet, I thought I heard—

Griselda (listening)

No—no one—blonds are tender—chestnut would be even better—he would be tender and passionate—Great God!—a sudden fear has come over me—suppose he is a redhead—we haven't foreseen that.

Doña Beatrix

There's knocking at the door to the secret staircase—my heart is beating horribly.

(Quickly Griselda goes to open. Don Gaspar enters, accompanied by a page.)

Griselda

Enter—Señor, cavalier.

Doña Beatrix (to page)

Take this, page, and be discreet.

(The page leaves.)

Don Gaspar (aside)

Where am I—? Who do I see—? Doña Beatrix.

Doña Beatrix (aside)

I'm trembling.

Griselda (aside)

This cavalier has a nice face—come on—chance has done things very nicely.

Don Gaspar (bowing)

Señora—

Doña Beatrix (bowing)

Señor!

Don Gaspar

Who's promised me this unhoped for joy of seeing you?— Happiness must be accepted without questions I don't dare to imagine—

Doña Beatrix

The Queen has directed us to tell you that she will not forget the one who was so courageously devoted to her. Elizabeth of Parma will not be an ingrate.

Don Gaspar

Am I not already greatly rewarded?

Doña Beatrix (aside)

What's he saying? Could it be me he loves? I was afraid of not pleasing him!

Don Gaspar

But for this fortunate event which brings us together— would the dearest wish of my soul ever be realized?— To see you, speak to you: that was my whole ambition—

Doña Beatrix

Oh, sir—

Don Gaspar

Ah! If I obtained a look from you, by saving a queen, I would save all the queens in the worlds, and if I had a hundred lives I would risk them one after the other.

Griselda

Ta, ta, ta! Did you recite that all pure from Diane de Montemayor?

These lovers have the mania of speaking only in the phrases of a novel—you don't need—Señor Tall-Dark-and-Handsome—to pretend to the heart of the Señora—to run through giants and cut off the heads of enchanters—she has promised her hand and her fortune to the valiant chevalier who flew to the rescue of the Queen!

Don Gaspar

What do I hear—? Am I lucky enough to—?

Doña Beatrix

Griselda has told you the truth—

Don Gaspar

It's a dream—! A beautiful dream—mine, your hand, mine, your love.

Griselda

We are not girls to let our word be protested.

Doña Beatrix

Aren't you the savior of the Queen?

Don Gaspar

Yes, Señora!—yes! Oh, my good angel who made me take this path, thanks! Just now, Doña Beatrix, I was wandering, unfortunately, proscribed. The wheel of my fortune, pushed by you, has turned, and I pass from shadow to light, from tears, to joy—from despair to happiness—a word from you—to a passing stranger who has made him the most enviable man in all Spain.— Almost a god. It's actually true? I am here—in front of you! No magic illusion is playing with me. I see—through your beauty, your charming soul smiles, encouraged by this celestial indulgence.

I can hope, I can believe— Oh, no—it's not possible! There's going to be some fatal awakening here. That I am loved by you, that you will be my wife, and it's not fever or folly that prattles on my lips—!

I fall at your knees—you are not repulsing me— This hand that my delirium dares to press—you are not wrathfully withdrawing it? My kisses glide over it—and what have I done, Great God—to deserve such happiness?— You still let me—!

Doña Beatrix

I promised it to the savior of the Queen, Don Melchior.

Don Gaspar (rising, aside)

Don Melchior—what's it mean? She takes me for another!

Doña Beatrix

What's wrong with you?

Griselda

You've gone pale!

Don Gaspar

Oh—! That's nothing.

(aside)

Don Melchior—! What mystery!

Doña Beatrix

Are you uneasy—troubled?—Are you thinking of the danger that threatens you?

Don Gaspar

No, Señora, no—!

Doña Beatrix

Relax! The Queen takes great interest in your fate—I'm rushing to inform her you've arrived without mishap.

Griselda

Go, Señora, and meanwhile count on me to fulfill the duties of hospitality.

Doña Beatrix

Well—I am leaving you, Don Melchior—and you aren't saying anything to me?

Don Gaspar

I love you—

Griselda

Marvelous! Now leave—a woman cannot ask for more.

(Beatrix leaves)

Don Gaspar (aside)

I really knew it couldn't all be true—I can only be

happy under the name of another.

Griselda

Well—Señor Melchior—spoiled child of Fortune?

Don Gaspar

Yes, you said it, Griselda, spoiled child of Fortune.

(aside)

O bloody irony of destiny!

Griselda

Confess that you've had insolent, good luck! Instead of being hanged, as is your right, you are going to marry a charming woman—instead of coursing through hill and dale with the Alguazils on your heels, you are hidden in the very castle of Aranjuez, in the room of Señora Griselda, a very sought-after fate—instead of gnawing a piece of black bread in an isolated hole—you have in prospect a fine repast.

Don Gaspar

I'm not hungry.

Griselda

Come off it! Your infanta is no longer here—don't

make so much ceremony. Only young girls of eighteen imagine that a lover lives on the tune of a guitar.

Don Gaspar

I thank you—

Griselda

Eat like an ogre— That won't prevent me from thinking you are the most passionate cavalier in two worlds— Shall I serve you a La Mancha ham, cured with sugar?

Don Gaspar

You are thousand times too kind—! I don't want a thing—

Griselda

If you aren't hungry, at least you must be thirsty— here's some sherry wine.

(Don Melchior enters through the window.)

Griselda

Great God!

Don Gaspar

A man!

Don Melchior (aside)

Alguazil curs! No other way to escape them!

(aloud)

A thousands pardons. I am disturbing a private conversation.

Griselda

Two cavaliers in my bedroom at night! What a scandal—! And there I was husbanding my reputation to get married at Easter.

(going to Melchior)

Who are you?

Don Melchior (aside)

Watch it! It would be dangerous to make myself known.

Griselda (to Don Gaspar)

Protect me!

Don Gaspar

Don't worry.

(to Don Melchior)

Exactly who are you?

Don Melchior

Once more, a thousand pardons. Perhaps—I am indiscreet—I arrive here like an intruder— But don't worry—I am not a thief— Look at me—I don't think I seem like one—

Don Gaspar (taking him aside)

By chance would you be the gallant of this young girl?

Don Melchior

I rather was thinking it was you.

Don Gaspar

You enter her place through the window.

Don Melchior

You are staying at the place after midnight.

Griselda (aside)

What are they saying?

Don Gaspar (to Griselda)

I know how to behave, my beautiful child!

Griselda

Well—

Don Gaspar

Trust yourself to my discretion.

Griselda

Huh? What's that mean?

Don Melchior

Count on my silence.

Don Gaspar

This cavalier is undoubtedly your fiancée.

Griselda

What an idea!

Don Melchior

This gentleman is, no doubt, your lover.

Griselda

What horror!

Don Gaspar

I don't wish to pry. I'm going to write to her.

(aside)

It's necessary—"To Doña Beatrix"

(He sits and writes at a table to the side.)

Griselda (aside)

What's he doing, good God?

Don Melchior (to Griselda)

What do I see? I, who wanted so much to eat— Be as nice as you are pretty—and allow me to sup.

(He goes to sit at the other side.)

Griselda

Well! Well! What are you doing?—Unheard of—!

Don Melchior

Don't get enraged—I am only taking a small slice of pâté.

(He fills his plate.)

Griselda

A little slice! He serves himself like a Monk!

Don Gaspar (aside)

I cannot hesitate: I must reveal my name to Doña Beatrix—

Ah! This letter is too cold.

(He tears it up.)

Don Melchior (drinking)

This wine is delicious!

Griselda

Well— Don't be shy!

Don Melchior

Excuse me!— Just a small drop.

(He fills his glass.)

Griselda

A small drop! He drinks like a Templar!

Don Gaspar

(Aside, tearing up another letter.)

That one's too hot!

Griselda (to Melchior)

I suppose that you are not going to remain around here all night?

Don Melchior

I wouldn't complain about it.

Griselda

You'll ruin me—I have only my virtue and—300 piastres. Get out! I have duties to complete—I am a girl of the bed-chamber to Her Majesty, and I aspire to become a Lady of Honor.

Don Melchior

Ah! So much the better—I am going to confide a delicate and mysterious mission to you— Will you do it—?

Griselda

If it convinces you to leave.

Don Melchior

You are very nice.

(Rising)

You know Doña Beatrix?

Don Gaspar (aside)

What's he say?

Griselda

Yes! Well?

Don Melchior

Go tell her that I'm waiting for her here.

Don Gaspar

(Rising aside)

What do I hear?

Griselda

Why you—?

Don Melchior

The one she loves!

Don Gaspar (aside)

Head and blood!

Griselda (aside)

I'm no longer following him!

Don Gaspar

Go, Griselda, leave us—I must speak to this cavalier.

Don Melchior

What's he want with me?

(To Griselda)

Go, mercy—here's some money.

Don Gaspar (to Griselda)

Here's some money— Don't let her come—

Griselda

I'm on my way—I'm rushing—my gracious gentlemen.

(Aside, shaking a purse in each hand)

Right—for an honest girl here's a night of good things.

(She leaves)

Don Gaspar

You are loved by Doña Beatrix?

Don Melchior

I'm not exactly hated— But let's break this off—don't lead me into fatuity.

Don Gaspar

And, no doubt, you have very powerful titles to that love.

Don Melchior

I don't wish to boast—that's not my custom—but beyond the physical and moral accomplishments that people are pleased to observe in me—I have indeed some rights over the heart of this charming Señora—

Don Gaspar

Rights?

Don Melchior

Yes—something like a vow—like a promise—in the end—sufficient— The adventure is romantic enough.

Don Gaspar

And may one know it?

Don Melchior

Oh! No—it's too much to my advantage.

Don Gaspar

Try to do violence to your modesty.

Don Melchior

I let others recount things like that—a gallant man never speaks of his powers—I have a horror of boasting—

Don Gaspar

I am like you—but one can simply recount what one has done that's good.

Don Melchior

Sing one's own panegyric— That's in poor taste—but it's not my fault if I only do acts of valor, with marks of sublime devotion and intrepidity.

Don Gaspar

That condemns you to complete silence?

Don Melchior

You are Castilian?

Don Gaspar

Yes—

Don Melchior

Honest?

Don Gaspar

No one has ever doubted it—

Don Melchior

Discreet?

Don Gaspar

Like a tomb!

Don Melchior

That's good. I confide myself to this—lugubrious comparison. I actually intend, vis-à-vis you, to depart from my ordinary modest reserve.

(louder)

This very day at 4:15—as you see me—I committed a

heroic action.

Don Gaspar

Of what type?

Don Melchior

The type of ancient paladins—but perfected.

Don Gaspar

I didn't think there was still an Amadis under Philippe V!

Don Melchior-

There are some! You've heard of the event that happened to the Queen?

Don Gaspar

Like everybody.

(aside)

Where's he coming from?

Don Melchior

An event that did not have funereal consequences, thanks to the devotion of a savior—

Don Gaspar

Who remains unknown. I know —

Don Melchior

And this savior whose name no one knows—

Don Gaspar

You know him?

Don Melchior

By Jove!

Don Gaspar

What do you mean?

Don Melchior

'Twas I!

Don Gaspar

(Stupefied)

You!

Don Melchior

Yes!

Don Gaspar

Now that is strange!

Don Melchior

Nothing is more simple. I was passing by there—I stopped the horse.

Don Gaspar

Are you quite sure of that?

Don Melchior

Bizarre question!

Don Gaspar

Not so bizarre!

Don Melchior

I have no doubt about my identity.

Don Gaspar

I have mine.

Don Melchior

Do I have an untruthful appearance?

Don Gaspar

Fabulous!

Don Melchior

Thus they call the period which precedes historic times. Is it your intention to apply this epithet to me in a disagreeable sense?

Don Gaspar

For the sense that will displease you. You are not the man who saved the Queen.

Don Melchior

Why?

Don Gaspar

Because—I will tell you—sword in hand.

Don Melchior

But, still—

Don Gaspar

Come on, let's go—

Don Melchior

Listen—

Don Gaspar

I'm not going to listen to a thing. To the fountain of Cybele.

Don Melchior

What! At night?

Don Gaspar

There's enough moonlight to chastise a scoundrel!

Don Melchior

Scoundrel!

Don Gaspar

Let's march!

Don Melchior

Instantly— But so as not to awaken suspicious, let's each arrive separately at the meeting place.

Don Gaspar

Agreed! We will reach the gardens of the palace more

swiftly using this secret stairway.

(goes to the door at the left)

Pass—

Don Melchior

After you—

Don Gaspar

I beg you—

Don Melchior

I won't do it! Two gentlemen can cut each other's throats, but cannot fail in the laws of civility.

Don Gaspar

Let's go!

Don Melchior

Let's go.

(They again bow to each other, Don Gaspar ends by leaving first, Don Melchior at first takes a step to follow him, and suddenly locks the door)

Don Melchior (alone)

Bully! Ruffian! What a furious type! Could he be a husband in the category of the late Menelaus? Go wait for me under the beautiful stars! I'm in no hurry to get carved up. This braggart picks his time ill. I have no envy to fight a duel when I'm on the eve of marrying Doña Beatrix—seductive fiancée—rich like a treasure ship—I intend at least to undertake the conquest of this pretty-faced millionaire and virgin—two precious qualities—but rare. She cannot fail to come after receiving my gallant message. By Jove! She adores me before having seen me— What will she do after she does? A woman!

(A door opens and the Queen appears.)

Queen

Is it you, Don Melchior?

Don Melchior (aside)

It's she.

(aloud)

Don Melchior Claudio Narcissio Figueiro de Sandoval y Carvajal Peralta Hernández de Bovadilla— You guessed it—it's myself. I bear with as little as I can these names that have linked me to my ancestors.

Queen

I am meeting you, at last— How happy I am.

(Don Melchior pulls up a chair for her.)

Don Melchior

Lovely person; charming character.

Queen

I can express my sentiments to you regarding you.

(Don Melchior sits near the Queen, she makes a motion of surprise)

Don Melchior (aside)

I've produced my customary effect. She idolizes me.

Queen

I regard you as the most perfect gentleman that ever can be.

Don Melchior

One of the most perfect would suffice, Señora—my humility suffers from such praise.

Queen

You've shown a devotion that was heroic, chivalrous—divine.

Don Melchior

I have but one virtue—that's modesty—your praise is going to ruin it—spare me—mercy—

Queen

El Cid himself couldn't have done better.

Don Melchior

He would have done as well. Grant me that or I will be forced to blush. I appreciate what I am worth.

Queen

Noble and generous young man! To come to the aid of the Queen, you didn't hesitate to brave death and the scaffold. How to reward such a fine action?

Don Melchior

The action wasn't bad, I agree since you insist on it—I am not teasing. As for the reward, I will content myself with the impression I dare flatter myself to have produced on your heart.

Queen (rising)

On my heart! What does this extravagance signify?

Don Melchior

You are beautiful and I am a hero—you said so just now, for I am incapable of giving myself such denominations—beauty must crown valor!

Queen

Don Melchior!

Don Melchior

Never has the myrtle of love been placed on a more submissive face. You have vanquished the invincible— my soul is yours—

Queen (aside)

The wretch—was it for me then that he insinuated himself into the Park of Aranjuez?

Don Melchior

O my star! I thank you! There was only one way to please her and you gave it to me— The savior of the Queen—they tell me—has all possible rights to your favor.

Queen

To my favor—I don't deny it.

Don Melchior

To your esteem.

Queen

No question! He deserved it. But just now you employed language to me that—

Don Melchior

Did I use improper terms? Have I committed some grammatic offense? It seems to me I employed only honest words and respectful formulas—to outrage modesty is not my custom.

Queen (aside)

Now this is peculiar!

(aloud)

Sir, be careful!—I don't know if you are joking or speaking seriously—but you are playing a hazardous game—such insolence—that nothing authorizes.

Don Melchior

To tell a pretty woman that one loves her has never passed for insolence—especially if the declaration is given a graceful turn—and mine—

Queen

Oh—shut up—

Don Melchior

Why—

Queen

Not another word! Anyone else would already have been punished—but your bravery pleads for your folly—a trait I cannot forget suspends my wrath.

Don Melchior

You see in me the most speechless cavalier on earth—I fall from my height—I no longer understand a thing—the manner in which you are greeting me causes me profound stupefaction. I express to you delicate feelings in a flowery style I dare say—poetic— I accompany my speech with gestures in good taste and you seem indignant, outraged as if a man dressed in out-of-fashion and threadbare clothes, with clumsy hands, had the audacity to meddle in your conversation. What in me can shock you? Don't I have cultivated manners? Irreproachable dress—facile speech—but pure? Perhaps, I haven't from respect—depicted my tenderness under sufficiently vivid colors—? No! I do not love you—get back—languishing words—too cold expressions—I adore you—I idolize you—my head is burning, my heart flames—I am just a vast conflagration!

Queen

Wretch!

Don Melchior

I am throwing myself at your feet—I'm dragging myself to your knees—I kiss the tracks of your steps.

Queen

Fool—

Don Melchior

What's got to be said—What must be done to calm you?

Queen

Come to your senses—and leave— Thanks to your devotion, I actually intend to regard you merely as a madman.

Don Melchior

Mad with love.

Queen

Don't irritate me further—I will try to forget this moment of delirium—I pity you—

Don Melchior

You pity me? In that case—

Queen (starting to leave)

Thank me for so much clemency—

Don Melchior

You are fleeing? Oh! I am going to pursue you!

Queen

Remember well, sir, if you again use such bold language to me—it's death that awaits you—

Don Melchior

Death?

Queen

Death!

(She leaves)

Don Melchior (alone)

Death?—that conclusion lacks kindness. What's it mean? Could she have a handy knife in her virginal garter? I remain paralyzed—so greatly am I struck by surprise! There are two things I'll never comprehend: the Apocalypse and women! This one declares herself a fanatic about the queen's savior. I present myself as such—and the capricious creature casts thunderous glances of rage and disdain at me!

Ah—who's that?

(Don Gaspar enters)

Don Melchior

The hired killer again. We are going to cut each other up like two dividers—it's become inevitable.

Don Gaspar

I've been waiting for you for an hour at the rendez-vous!

Don Melchior

I wanted to allow you time to commend your soul to God.

Don Gaspar

This time you won't escape me.

(He casts away his cloak and his hat.)

Don Melchior

What are you doing?

Don Gaspar (hand on his sword.)

These torches will give us better light than the stars. Come on! Draw!

Don Melchior

What an enragé! I don't fight with no exit.

Don Gaspar

Watch out! I'll force you to if you have courage.

Don Melchior

Dueling is punished by death, think about it carefully!

Don Gaspar

You're getting pale, valiant hero.

Don Melchior (aside)

What an unchained tiger— How to impose on him? Let's assume the manners of a captain!

Don Gaspar

You are trembling, dubious conqueror!

Don Melchior

No, by all the saints! You know ill Don Melchior de Bovadilla. If I touch—he's a dead man—if I come down, it's on the bold—if I advance, these are my conquests—if I write, it's a challenge—if I read, it's a death warrant—if I win, it's a battle—if I ruin, they are my enemies; if I enter, it's through the breach—if I emerge, it's from combat.

Don Gaspar

No idle words.

Don Melchior

Bold man! I intend to spare you in the interest of your mistress and you push me to extremes. One explains oneself before cutting each others' throats—and you are not telling me why you want to cross swords?

Don Gaspar

Why? We both love the same woman!

Don Melchior

Ah? Bah!

Don Gaspar

Doña Beatrix d'Astorga.

Don Melchior

Doña Beatrix—

(aside)

It's this braggart who has stolen her heart from me!

(The Count enters abruptly.)

Count de San Lucas

You here, my nephew?

Don Melchior (aside)

True God! He comes perfectly.

Count de San Lucas

I learned you were here, I'm rushing to congratulate

you.

Don Melchior

Me?

Count de San Lucas

The Queen by the power of her solicitations has obtained mercy for her savior.

Don Gaspar (aside)

Let's listen. This interests me.

Don Melchior

Hooray! I will not be cut down in the flower of my youth.

Count de San Lucas

The most beautiful future awaits you. The Queen will answer for making you succeed. Do you have ambition, young man?

Don Melchior

Sure!

Count de San Lucas

Great!

Don Melchior

I would like to be a Marquis.

Count de San Lucas

You will perhaps become chamberlain—camerero.

Don Melchior

Chamberlain! Camerero! That idea exalts me!

Count de San Lucas

Fortune is smiling on you, listen I've just seen Doña Beatrix.

Don Gaspar (aside)

Attention! That interests me, also.

Don Melchior

Don't joke, uncle.

Count de San Lucas

I never joke. I am Castilian and grave. Why, Don Melchior! You've turned the head of your cousin!

Don Gaspar (aside)

What do I hear—! It was me she took for him?

Don Melchior

This time, you are jesting, uncle.

Count de San Lucas

I never jest, I tell you. I am grave and Castilian.

Don Melchior

Doña Beatrix displays an indifference to me—

Count de San Lucas

She affirms a tenderness for you.

Don Gaspar (aside)

This is delightful to hear.

Don Melchior

She can't stand me.

Count de San Lucas

She's going crazy about you—

Don Gaspar (aside)

My happiness is becoming intoxicating.

Don Melchior

I can only repeat to you: no.

Count de San Lucas

And as for me, I will prove to you—it's yes.

Don Melchior

Ah! Why—I ask nothing better!

Don Gaspar (aside)

And what about me!

Don Melchior (to Don Gaspar)

You hear him?

Don Gaspar

Perfectly.

Count de San Lucas (to Don Melchior, showing him a ring.)

You see this ring?

Don Melchior

Well—?

Count de San Lucas (givng it to him)

She sends it to you as a pledge of Love.

Don Melchior

To me! She loves me!

Don Gaspar (aside)

To me! She adores me!

Don Melchior (to Don Gaspar)

You hear him!

Don Gaspar

As well as you!

Count de San Lucas (to Don Melchior)

Do you still doubt her feelings? Is it clear enough? What do you say about that?

Don Melchior

I was too modest!

Don Gaspar (aside)

What an ass!

Don Melchior

She acted so cruel!

Count de San Lucas

Pure comedy.

Don Melchior

I will take my revenge. I will force this Amazon to surrender her weapons to me.

Count de San Lucas

Come join her at the ball.

Don Melchior

Yes, let's run to the ball!

Count de San Lucas

Don't let yourself be intimidated: women have so many caprices—whims— Be enterprising—like a page.

Don Melchior

Like a page.

Count de San Lucas

Bold like a gallant knight.

Don Melchior

I have my own notion—come, uncle.

Don Gaspar (retaining him)

Excuse me—we have a conversation to finish.

Don Melchior

He calls a duel a conversation—! Frightful ruffian!

Count de San Lucas

That's different. I am leaving you, gentleman—

Don Melchior

Stay, uncle—

Count de San Lucas

Impossible! My duty as general Master of Ceremonies demands my presence at the ball. Till later, Melchior. I am a complaisant uncle—I will bring you Beatrix's hand for the first minuet!

(He leaves)

Don Melchior

You still want to kill me?

Don Gaspar

Much less than before.

Don Melchior

This is no doubt a joke.

Don Gaspar

Why?

Don Melchior

You are unlucky in women—

Don Gaspar

Who knows? Don't yell "victory" yet. I retained you to give you a friend's advice— Renounce Doña Beatrix.

Don Melchior

Didn't you hear that she breathes only for me?

Don Gaspar

That proves nothing!

Don Melchior

And this ring she sent me?

Don Gaspar

The wisdom of nations advises us not to be confident of appearances.

Don Melchior

Are you deaf?

Don Gaspar

I am the happiest of men.

Don Melchior

Are you mad?

Don Gaspar

Doña Beatrix will soon belong to me.

Don Melchior

She already belongs to me.

Don Gaspar

Don't dispute her with me.

Don Melchior

You must let me have her.

Don Gaspar

Trust me!

Don Melchior

Don't persist further!

Don Gaspar

This is madness!

Don Melchior

This is bull-headedness!

(Griselda enters)

Griselda

What's this uproar in my place—you again, gentlemen?

Don Gaspar

Griselda, I am swimming in fog.

Don Melchior

Griselda, I'm in an ocean of happiness.

Don Gaspar

Holy Virgin, what is it?

Don Melchior

To me, her fortune.

Don Gaspar

To me, her love.

Griselda

It's Doña Beatrix who's making you rave like this. I suspected as much.

Don Gaspar

The pearl of Castile.

Don Melchior

The star of the court.

Don Gaspar

I am going to possess her.

Don Melchior

I am going to obtain her.

Griselda

What, the two of you!

Don Gaspar

My happiness intoxicates me.

Don Melchior

My joy transports me.

Don Gaspar

One last time, renounce the one who I love!

Don Melchior

One last time, think no more of my lover.

Don Gaspar

She prefers me.

Don Melchior

She's marrying me.

Don Gaspar

By Saint John! Enough talking like women. We must act like men.

(Drawing his sword)

Griselda

Holy Virgin! Help! Let's run find the Alguazils.

Don Melchior (aside)

I'm done for! I'm dead and burned.

Don Gaspar

En garde!

Don Melchior (drawing his sword)

(aside)

Let's make a good appearance— The Alguazils will separate us.

Don Gaspar

At last!

Don Melchior

Yes, at last, but not yet—! I am of an ancient race—my nobility date from the Ostrogoths—and I do not fight with the first comer. Who are you?

Don Gaspar

I promised to tell you sword in hand; I am Captain Gaspar! Yes, the true savior of the Queen.

Don Melchior

Why then, wretch! I am ruined—sunk—if I don't kill you?

Don Gaspar

Try!

Don Melchior (aside)

Perplexing situation.

Don Gaspar

My life or yours.

Don Melchior

Hold on! Hold on! Let us make with our swords all the greetings that urbane Castilian manners exact.

(They fence in a comic way at first. They cross swords and just exchange some thrusts when Griselda appears with the Alguazils.)

Griselda

Stop, come—come this way, you Alguazils!

Don Gaspar (aside)

Let's avoid the laws against dueling.

(aloud, staggering)

Wounded— Ah! I am dying!

(he falls as if dead.)

Don Melchior (aside)

I killed him! How to escape, then?

(aloud)

Struck through the heart!

(staggers)

This is my last moment.

(he falls as if dead)

Griselda

Both dead! Mercy!

Head of the Alguazils

We arrive too late. We must inform the mayor—the alcalde.

(The Alguazils leave.)

Griselda

(Falling into an armchair.)

Now here's a nice how-do-you-do. Two bodies in my room—and after midnight—! Scandal will, perhaps, say they are living.

Don Melchior (rising)

I have that advantage over my enemy.

Griselda (uttering a scream and rising)

Just heaven! What a scare you gave me—you are the conqueror!

Don Melchior

I am the invincible.

(Picking up his sword and addressing Don Gaspar.)

You are dead, audacious fellow! Ah—how big he is, and I'm the one who killed him! Let's go now and fascinate Doña Beatrix—I no longer fear to proclaim myself savior of the Queen to the face of Europe.

(He leaves proudly, hat on his ear.)

Griselda (kneeling near Gaspar.)

Poor young man!

(Don Gaspar kisses her hand; Griselda rises with a scream)

Great God! You are not dead?

Don Gaspar

The dead don't go to a ball, and I'm heading there.

(He picks up his sword, takes his hat and his cloak.)

Griselda

To seek out your rival again?

Don Gaspar

No—rather, my fiancée. Guide me into the palace, Griselda.

Griselda (taking him by the hand.)

Let's avoid the Alguazils—this way, my hero, this way.

(She drags him to the door of the hidden stairway—after a moment the mayor-alcalde and the Alguazils appear at the door.)

CURTAIN

ACT III
THE THIRD DAY

A ballroom giving on splendid illuminated gardens.

Doña Beatrix

Why, he was charming, the monster—but it's he that was speaking to me with an air of sincerity, the liar! Everyone will be deceived by it. Who will believe henceforth if the voice that says, "I love you," is a lying voice—and if the eye that passion seems to illuminate renders itself an accomplice in the imposture?

Queen

Dear innocent, I can see you don't know the ways of our young folks of fine manners. Don Melchior is one of those asses of the worst sort. At the same time he was pursuing you with his banal protestations, he had the incomparable boldness to speak to me of love— ME—The Queen of Spain—

Doña Beatrix

The traitor! For that audacious sacrilege, he deserves to be burned at the next auto-de-fé! I am sweet, I am nice, but such conduct screams out for vengeance.

Queen

I've shown too much patience. I ought to have warned the King. Because of you, I've been more indulgent than my dignity permits, but since you are no longer interested in Don Melchior, don't worry; he will be punished. I am going to complain to Don Philippe.

Doña Beatrix

To Don Philippe! Good God, Madame, oh, don't do it. The King would regard this outrage as a crime.

Queen

Console yourself, my tearful beauty, I am going to grant your request— The criminal is very dear to you, and the punishment would fall on you. Your smitten heart has not ceased to beat for Don Melchior.

Doña Beatrix

Ah! Señora! I will prove to you that Beatrix d'Astorga has plenty of pride and blushes for this weakness.

Queen

What are you going to do?

Doña Beatrix

I am rushing to find the Count de San Lucas to inform him of the odious conduct of his nephew—and to make plain to him that I renounce the hand of a dishonest gentleman.

(She leaves)

Queen (alone)

It's useless to deny it, Beatrix, Don Melchior is still dear to you. Well—! My capacity as queen is not going to make me forget the duties of a friend. I intended to bring back to you this ingrate who is abandoning you by means of prudent advice.

Don Melchior (entering)

I've messed up the steps of a dance, I've knocked over a platter of sorbets, I've disturbed an amorous private conversation, I've absorbed three flasks of sherry, and I've tread on the foot of the Grand Inquisitor who apologized to me. Such is my impatience to find my lover! Here she is. Let's change our approach. Perhaps that will succeed for me. We shall pass from boldness to timidity.

Queen

It's him!

Don Melchior

She's noticed me. Let's utter some sighs made to turn the head of a young girl.

Queen

What a languishing air!

Don Melchior

Oh!

Queen

Don Melchior.

Don Melchior

It's you who speak to, me, Señora. Alas! I don't even dare raise my eyes to you.

Queen

That's about right.

Don Melchior

Don't worry anymore that I will address the least word

to you which may seem inconvenient.

Queen

Better and better.

Don Melchior

I feel too well the respect I owe a person of your birth, of your rank.

Queen

There now—you see you've become better behaved—and you are right, my young cavalier—

(aside)

Let's speak to him of Doña Beatrix.

(aloud)

Don't you know that there's a woman in the world who thinks only of you?

Don Melchior (aside)

Charming confession in a charming mouth.

Queen

Is it necessary to unveil the depth of her feelings

regarding you—?

Don Melchior

Unveil, Señora, unveil!

Queen

Well—! She experiences towards you the most lively sympathy.

Don Melchior

And it's you who tell me that?

Queen

Myself—

Don Melchior

Why then—I cannot doubt it—

Queen

Why, certainly—!

Don Melchior

Ah! Señora—had I but known it sooner—

Queen

You would not have addressed a certain speech to me.

Don Melchior

Assuredly not—I would have spared myself the expense of useless elocution.

Queen

Think carefully, Don Melchior, that it's up to you to become the happiest of men—what is lacking to your happiness? You are going to have a lovable, gracious, charming wife.

Don Melchior (aside)

For goodness sake! She's got a nice enough opinion of herself.

Queen

I would actually say witty—

Don Melchior

I will teach her to be more modest.

Queen

And I will add, at last, that she loves you.

Don Melchior

I hear you with ecstasy.

Queen

It's she herself who speaks to you with my voice.

Don Melchior

No doubt, Señora, no doubt—

Queen

She says to you: renounce at once all the disorders that have plagued your youth. She says to you: it's time to seek a calmer, more intimate happiness—this happiness I am here to offer you.

(Griselda appears without being seen by the characters on stage.)

Queen

What's the use of all your mad intrigues? What woman in the world can love you like me?

Griselda

What do I hear?

Queen

Have good hope. I have no more threats to make you. I can forget a moment of distraction, and I take it upon myself to promise you life and happiness.

Don Melchior (hurling himself to the feet of the Queen.)

Allow me, in that case, Señora.

Griselda (holding him)

Stop. What are you going to do? Look—but don't touch.

(Exit the Queen)

Don Melchior

What's it mean?

(aside)

Marvelous! I can say, like Caesar—I came, I was seen, I conquered.

Griselda

This gentleman seems to me to be on a fine path— Let's get in his good graces—Milord.

Don Melchior

Who's speaking to me?

Griselda

It is I, little Griselda, that Milord deigned to compromise last night by scaling her balcony—I am very proud of having received your Excellency in my room—

Don Melchior

Truly?

Griselda

I glory in having given supper to Your Highness.

Don Melchior

Highness—Excellency, this sort of adulation resembles flattery.

Griselda

Ah! You are a very lucky man, indeed— That's what it is to be bold!

Don Melchior

I was bold? Where? Who? How?

Griselda

I will keep my mouth shut, Milord. I understand that you don't wish to entrust me with a secret of this importance—almost a state secret.

Don Melchior (aside)

A state secret? What's she saying? Ah—There's a secret.

(aloud)

And you saw? You heard?

Griselda

Hush!

Don Melchior

Hush?

(aside)

I'd really like to know.

(aloud)

And you won't tell anyone?

Griselda

Trust yourself to me, Milord.

Don Melchior

Entirely. But since we are alone—and no one can hear us—tell me without fear and without subterfuge—what you saw, and—

Griselda

Hush!

Don Melchior

Hush?

Griselda

That lady to whom you were speaking of love—

Don Melchior

Well?

Griselda

Well—what she replied to you—

Don Melchior

She replied to my tenderness.

Griselda

You find that quite natural?

Don Melchior

Yes, indeed!

Griselda

Then you are accustomed to turn the head of Infantas and of Empresses—!

Don Melchior

What do you mean? It's neither a question of an Infanta, nor a Empress—

Griselda

Hush!

Don Melchior

Hush?

Griselda

You are right—she's neither an Infanta, nor an Empress—

Don Melchior.

She is—see—

(At this moment, the Queen, crown on her head, passes at the back, lords and ladies bowing as she passes. Griselda leaves.)

Don Melchior (alone)

She's the queen, the Queen of Spain and The Indies! A chair, an armchair, a sofa. I am annihilated, petrified, my blood is freezing—my hair standing on end— I'm experiencing a convulsive trembling, a shattering panic—I'm done for—I threw myself at her feet. I wanted to kiss her hand—I wanted to take her—

—and she didn't call her guard—she didn't deliver me to the Inquisitor! Saints of heaven— This clemency is significant enough. But still, I cannot imagine—all vain, all vain—my modesty doesn't make yours—if you please. Then deliver yourself to the evidence— what the devil—it's clear enough, it seems to me. Come on, decidedly, Bovadilla, you are a great man and I am forced to admire you—even though it costs me— This is going to restore somewhat my reputation as a conqueror which began to lower! Favorite of the Queen—superb political position—and gastronomical as well—I will make ministers and five meals a day.

I will sell positions to the highest bidder, but I will only grant the position of chef to real merit— Favorite of the Queen—now there's my real vocation—if I haven't made anything of myself.

It's because I was good only for this—monarchic position. First of all, I'll make myself Minister of Finances— that way I'll be able to pay my creditors. Ah! Fie, Melchior, prosperity is already beginning to make you stupid— Does one pay folks like that?— I intend to have in my cellars the most delicious French wines. In my stables the most magnificent Andalousians; moreover, a pack of English hounds to hunt the stag and a pack of poets to celebrate my perfections—

Count de San Lucas (entering)

Well! Melchior—well!—was I right, and your fiancée, Doña Beatrix—

Don Melchior

It is indeed a question of Doña Beatrix—I renounce her.

Count de San Lucas

What do I hear?

Don Melchior

Return this ring to her—

Count de San Lucas

Is it possible?

Don Melchior

She's only a maid of honor—

Count de San Lucas

Well?

Don Melchior

Don Melchior de Bovadilla aspires now to a more illustrious conquest. I cannot say more to you than that—I run—I fly to fortune on the path enameled with roses and—sensuality!

(He exits.)

Count de San Lucas

Well! Now what's wrong with him? Return this ring to Doña Beatrix— He's given me an agreeable task—it's she.

Doña Beatrix

Here he is! Uncle, I am very unhappy. Your nephew is the most perfidious of men.

Count de San Lucas

We are there.

Doña Beatrix

How I suffer—if you knew—! Have you ever loved?

Count de San Lucas

Often.

Doña Beatrix

Have you ever been deceived?

Count de San Lucas

Always.

Doña Beatrix

Then you understand what I'm enduring—a broken heart—I've just seen the Queen and she's unveiled to me the abominable conduct of Don Melchior.

It's a crime that has no name.

Count de San Lucas

A crime!

Doña Beatrix

Don Melchior dared to make—declarations to her—

Count de San Lucas

To the Queen?

Doña Beatrix

Yes—to the Queen!

Count de San Lucas

He forgot morality and etiquette—to that degree?

Doña Beatrix

But what do I see? I am not deceived! It's the ring that I charged you with for that flighty lover.

Count de San Lucas

Alas, my dear Beatrix, how to apprise you of this unworthy news—

Doña Beatrix

I divine it—Don Melchior is sending me back my ring—behold his Spanish gallantry!

Count de San Lucas (giving her the ring.)

It's the fatal truth!

Doña Beatrix

Ah—! I am humiliated enough! I really hope that Don Melchior will never reappear before me! And yet I would like to give it to him! Where is he, uncle, where is he?

Count de San Lucas

How you remind me! What an idea crosses my mind. You say that Don Melchior dares to love a certain person—I fear peeking into a horrible mystery—I am forming conjectures which make me shiver—

Doña Beatrix

Get to the point!

Count de San Lucas

No, no—more I cannot tell you—I run to watch—as my duty demands it.

Doña Beatrix

Watch what?

Count de San Lucas

The circulation of sorbets at the ball!

(He exits frantically.)

Doña Beatrix (alone)

What's he imagine? Oh! Men! Men! What deceivers they are! Don Melchior, what a cruel game have you played here! If you felt nothing for me, for what reason did you disguise your indifference in love, why ask on your knees for the hand you had no wish to obtain. It's him!

Don Gaspar (aside}

Doña Beatrix! Finally I have found her. Let's not delay to make this confession to her that honesty dictates I do—!

(aloud)

Señora—

Doña Beatrix

It's you, sir—you dare again offer yourself to my sight?

Don Gaspar

What change!

Doña Beatrix

You have sought this interview—It will be the last between us.

Don Gaspar

What do I hear?

Doña Beatrix

And by addressing an eternal goodbye to you, Doña Beatrix will have the sad satisfaction of expressing to you the feelings your odious conduct inspires in her!

Don Gaspar

What do you mean?

Doña Beatrix

You ought to understand—lover without honor—without delicacy, gentleman without fidelity. But I won't be the dupe any more of your fine sentiments of, your perfidious protestations—I know you too well now.

Don Gaspar

What are you saying? Have you discovered who I am?

Doña Beatrix

An ingrate, who sends me with disdain my engagement ring! An audacious man who actually dares to address his homage to his sovereign!

Don Gaspar

Me! Great God! Me!

Doña Beatrix

Ah—may I never see you again! Adieu forever, Don Melchior!

Don Gaspar

Stop! I can now reveal to you joyfully the name I bear—the name that just now I was fearfully going to reveal to you.

Doña Beatrix

Who are you?

Don Gaspar

Captain Don Gaspar—

Doña Beatrix

Don Gaspar—

Don Gaspar

A soldier of fortune who found himself garrisoned in Burgos, six months ago—and who noticed you for the first time through the grilled door of the choir at the monastery of Las Huelgas where you were being raised by your tutor. An obscure lover who, since that time spent many a feverish, insomniac night thinking of the uncrossable distance that separated him from you— A simple officer who loves you—but not at least, the gentleman who outrages you.

Doña Beatrix

You've loved me for such a long time?—and your reserve—your silence?

Don Gaspar

What could I hope? I silently tasted the sorrowful pleasure of an impossible passion—but my wound was so dear to me that I had no wish to be cured. Sometimes, there slid into my soul a vague and indefinable hope— Then I hastened to choke it back like a lying illusion, and even at this moment, don't think that I wish to abuse a promise that you made in a moment of exaltation, and which granted me rights to your hand.

Doña Beatrix

Ah!—there's an accent of truth in your words! But are

you aware that another also pretends—?

Don Gaspar

No, Señora! I will indeed know how to force him to retract—he who pretends to usurp your hand by the most odious imposture.

Doña Beatrix

Ah! Prove he is the sole imposter! Prove that you are the sole savior of the Queen!

Don Gaspar

How to do it?

Doña Beatrix

Prove it, and then, whoever you may be, the heiress of a noble Castilian house will not be a perjurer—mProve it—and this hand that you wouldn't want to owe to my pity, you will owe to my choice—to my love.

(aside)

Let's go apprise the Queen of my discovery.

(She leaves.)

Don Gaspar

Her hand! Her hand on that condition— And to fulfill it, to complete all my wishes—it's nothing more than an obstacle that I meet on my path—! This infernal Don Melchior—! Ah, I'll indeed know how to force him to admit he's an imposter.

Don Melchior

What a crowd! Impossible to meet the lady of my thoughts. Never mind. My debut at court surpasses all my hopes. And now one lone man can thwart my plans—it's Don Gaspar—but thanks to heaven and my butchering sword, he no longer exists!

Don Gaspar (tapping him on the shoulder.)

You are mistaken, Don Melchior.

Don Melchior

Believing my eyes? Captain Gaspar! Is it to you or to your ghost that I have the honor of speaking?

Don Gaspar

I am living—do you doubt it?

Don Melchior

Miraculous thing! You drowned in the Tagus and you

resuscitated. I ground you in the dust and you resuscitate. Have you contracted the habit of being reborn from your ashes like the Phoenix?

Don Gaspar

That annoys you, perhaps?

Don Melchior

Utterly—but I warn you I will no longer fight with you. I've given my proofs.

Don Gaspar

I will indeed force you to—

Don Melchior

I've given my proof! You will not force me. I already fought you once, I already killed you once—be reasonable: that ought to suffice for you. Undoubtedly you possess some talisman, some relic—? Some oriental amulet? A blessed scapulary, an enchanted ring of Great Merlin? Or a tooth of Saint Christopher?

Don Gaspar

You suspect my honesty?

Don Melchior

Well, no—but I intend to put it to the proof—I will no longer employ but a single weapon with you. You ask which? Sword, pistol, blunderbuss, crossbow, dagger, rapier, axe, or carbine. No—but persuasion— Confess that you are not the savior of the Queen!

Don Gaspar

For goodness's sake.

Don Melchior

Admit it—you will lose nothing by it—

Don Gaspar

Just the hand of Doña Beatrix.

Don Melchior

I cede her to you—I have in sight something other than my lover—that is to say, your lover—

Don Gaspar

Still.

Don Melchior

We are no longer rivals, Gaspar! Let's be friends,

Gaspar! Your hand, Gaspar— Let's hug each other, Gaspar—

Don Gaspar

What an original—

Don Melchior

I will protect you, Gaspar. I'm on such a fine path to arrive at a fortune. I am going to rise to a pinnacle—I will become minister, perhaps—I will topple Alberoni. But in the name of heaven allow me to proclaim myself the lone, the authentic savior of the Queen.

Count de San Lucas (enters)

Don Melchior, bad luck to you—I am myself charged with arresting you.

Don Melchior

O sudden reversal.

Count de San Lucas

The old law of Spain will be executed in all its rigor.

Don Melchior

I am not at my ease.

Count de San Lucas

The scaffold attends you.

Don Melchior

Yes, but I won't attend it. I am escaping as quickly as possible. Great God! Alguazils— Oh—this way—yet more Alaguazils! Why this side—there, too—I'm done for. I am surrounded on all sides!

Count de San Lucas

Don't be desolate, Melchior—you won't be hanged.

Don Melchior

I breathe easy.

Count de San Lucas

The antiquity of your race is opposed to that. You will be decapitated.

Don Melchior

I am not breathing easy.

Head of the Alguazils

Deliver your sword to me, Don Melchior.

Don Gaspar (coming forward)

It's mine alone that you must take.

Don Melchior

Castilian honor. I recognize you in such an act.

Don Gaspar

He's not this cavalier who touched the Queen—it was I.

Don Melchior

Spaniard from the time of Charles V—I admire you too much to contradict you.

Don Gaspar

It was I—and I am proving it by confessing to it at such a moment, before you gentlemen Alguazils, before you who hear me—to arrest me and punish me—

Queen (enters with Beatrix, Griselda, ladies, and gentlemen.)

The Queen too awaits you to reward you!

Don Melchior

The Queen.

Don Gaspar

Señora!

Queen

Fear nothing. It was a ruse, thanks to which we have finally discovered the truth. To you, Don Gaspar, all our benefits, all our gratitude. To you the hand of Doña Beatrix— As for you, Don Melchior—a perpetual prison—

Don Melchior

Pardon, Majesty— The desire to make myself illustrious— This need that great souls have—

Queen

Your boastfulness is the least of your crimes—but your audacity without name.

Don Melchior

Again, pardon, Majesty—I had only good intentions—I wanted to marry you—

Queen

You will go to the tower of Segovia—to meditate the worth of your words—

Don Melchior

O uncle—intercede for me.

Count de San Lucas

Leave me alone, sir—

Don Melchior

Unfortunate Don Melchior, abandoned by God and men—who will come to your aid?

Griselda

Me!

Don Melchior

I am then not abandoned by women?

Griselda

You entered my room through my window several minutes past midnight—an hour which always passes for very late. You owe me a dazzling reparation. I demand your hand.

Don Melchior

You demand my hand? Good Alguazils, drag me to the damp straw of dungeons.

Queen

Wait—Griselda's right. The honor of my servant must not even be suspected. We will pardon you on one condition—you will give your hand to this young girl—I insist on it—I'll take care of her dowry.

Don Melchior

Your Majesty orders, I obey. Long live the Queen!

All (music)

Long live the Queen—!

Queen

To the ball, gentlemen—

Don Melchior

Unfortunate Don Melchior! After having made a declaration to the Queen of Spain, he sent his ring back to Beatrix d'Astorga; now he marries a simple maid. What a melancholy fate.

(Then looks at her carefully.)

Ah, bah! She might have been ugly.

(He wants to kiss her.)

Griselda (pushing him away)

Before marriage, look—but don't touch.

CURTAIN

ALTERNATIVE ENDING
BY FRANK J. MORLOCK

All leave at a sign from The Queen except Don Melchior, who sits with his head in his hands.

After a moment the Queen appears in the doorway.

Queen

Don Melchior?

Don Melchior

Majesty?

(He rises quickly.)

Queen

Do you recollect what you said to me last night?

Don Melchior

Majesty, I—

Queen

Answer—!

Don Melchior

Yes—Majesty.

Queen

Did you mean those honeyed words—?

Don Melchior

Majesty, I—

Queen

Answer—!

Don Melchior

Yes, Majesty.

Queen

Then you admit—you dare to admit—

Don Melchior

I'd rather not admit—but I must—

Queen

In that case, Don Melchior—say them again—

(She smiles.)

Say them again—

Don Melchior (kneels at her feet.)

Queen!

Queen

No man has ever spoken to me like that. Say it again—

(She touches his head as Don Melchior begins to babble of love.)

CURTAIN

ABOUT THE TRANSLATOR

Frank J. Morlock has written and translated many plays since retiring from the legal profession in 1992. His translations have also appeared on Project Gutenberg, the Alexandre Dumas Père web page, Literature in the Age of Napoléon, Infinite Artistries.com, and Munsey's (formerly Blackmask). In 2006 he received an award from the North American Jules Verne Society for his translations of Verne's plays. He lives and works in México.

www.ingramcontent.com/pod-product-compliance
Lightning Source LLC
LaVergne TN
LVHW041626070426
835507LV00008B/470